# Phil H. LISTEMANN

**Colour artwork: Claveworks Graphic**

**Layout & project design: Phil Listemann**

Copyright © Philedition - Phil Listemann 2012

Printed in France

**ISBN: 978-2918590-49-1**

## ACKNOWLEDGEMENTS

William T. Larkins, Roger Wallsgrove (Text Consultant)

Edited and printed by Phil H. Listemann

*philedition@wanadoo.fr*

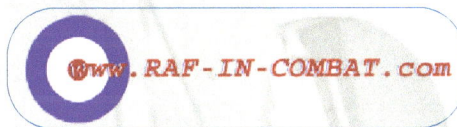

www.RAF-IN-COMBAT.com

## GLOSSARY OF TERMS

1c, 2c, 3c: First, Second and third Class
AMM: Aviation Machinist's Mate
AM: Aviation Metalsmith
ACRM: Aviation Chief Radioman
AP: Aviation Pilot
BAD: Base Air Detachment
BatFor: Battle Force
Del: Delivered
DBR: damaged beyond repair
Ens: Enseign

INA: Inspector of Naval Aviation
Lt (jg): Lieutenant (jg)
Lt-Cdm: Lieutenant-Commander
NAF: Naval Aircraft Factory
NRAB: Naval Reserve Aviation Base
NAS: Naval Air Station
OH: overhaul
RM: Radioman
Str.: Stricken from Navy list
TT: Total Time

# Grumman SF
# INTRODUCTION

The XSF-1 was basically a Grumman FF-1 modified for the scout role. Thus, the performance details were very similar.
*(National Archives)*

Less than three months after having ordering the prototype of the Grumman FF (see Allied Wings No.6), the Navy ordered another prototype to fulfil the scouting role from aircraft carriers on 9 June 1931 as the XSF-1 (Bu.No.8940). For Grumman, modifying the two-seat fighter into a two-seat scout aircraft was easy as the airframe permitted such modifications. Because Grumman moved from its Long Island facilities to new ones in New York State, the completion of prototype took more time than scheduled and the XSF-1 (model G-6 for Grumman) made its maiden flight on 20 August 1932. The XSF-1 was powered by the same engine installed on the FF-1, the Wright R-1820-78. The main difference between the XFF-1 and the XSF-1 was the deletion of the two forward guns to enable the internal fuel capacity to be increased from 120 to 165 US Gal. This was made possible by enlarging the tank located between the wheel wells. One of the two forward guns was replaced by one mounted in the starboard upper wing, and a flexible weapon of the same calibre installed in the rear cockpit. Two 100-lb bombs could also be carried beneath each of the lower wings. The XSF-1 was tested at Anacostia and tests proved satisfactory for the US Navy, the XSF-1 proved to be faster by 5 mph than the FF-1. An order for 34 SF-1s followed, deliveries started after the delivery of the last FF-1 to the USN and were completed by July 1934.

Wishing to avoid an increase in its staff, as the Grumman Corporation was at an early stage of its existence, Grumman decided to sub-contract Brewster to manufacture the wings and control surfaces. The SF-1s were different from the XSF-1 only in details, with a Wright R-1820-84 as engine (even if the very first ones were equipped with the -78 model). While under production, the contract was modified to convert the last ordered SF-1 into the XSF-2 prototype, which was powered with a Pratt & Whitney R-1535-72, the same engine installed on the XF2F-1. Receiving the Grumman designation of G-13, the XSF-2 had another main difference from the XSF-1 in having the forward-firing gun relocated on the right side of the cockpit. It was first flown on 26 November 1934, and had a top speed of 202 mph, meaning that the XSF-2 even though more powerful did not bring much advantage compared to the XSF-1 and no production SF-2 was ordered after the completion of the tests. However, the fact the XSF-2 remained unique in the USN inventory can be also explained by the wish of the USN not to look for anymore scout aircraft but scout-bombers instead, to optimise the limited space in aircraft-carriers. The XSF-2 was not a bad aircraft as such.

**One prototype XSF-1 Bu.No 8940 ordered in June 1931 by contract 21520.**

**8940**
*(c/n 102).* Acc. 14.06.33. Norfolk 25.09.33; Anacostia 27.09.33; NAF for fuel system modification date not recorded; Anacostia 08.01.34; Norfolk-VX185 for test; Anacostia 31.05.34; Norfolk date unrecorded; Anacostia date unrecorded; NAF 21.06.34; Anacostia 04.09.34; Grumman Co. 07.11.34; Wright Field Dayton 19.11.34; Anacostia 20.11.34; NAF for OH 22.01.35 completed 11.07.35; Anacostia 12.07.35; NAF for OH 05.08.35 completed 12.09.35; Anacostia 16.09.35; Norfolk for OH 04.05.36 completed 22.10.36; Anacostia 28.10.36; Norfolk for engine change (dash 84) date unrecorded complted 03.06.37; Anacostia 05.06.37, NAF for inspection 22.09.38.
**Str. 30.11.38** (1,125 TT).

## Deliveries and Strenght (SF-1)

| Month | Delivered | Total delivered | Acc. | Str. | On Hand |
|---|---|---|---|---|---|
| June 33 | 1 | 1 | - | - | **1** |
| .../... | | | | | |
| February 34 | 1 | 2 | - | - | **2** |
| March 34 | 3 | 5 | - | - | **5** |
| April 34 | 4 | 9 | - | - | **9** |
| May 34 | 11 | 20 | - | - | **20** |
| June | 8 | 28 | - | - | **28** |
| July 34 | 6 | 34 | - | - | **34** |
| August 34 | - | 34 | 1 | - | **33** |
| .../... | | | | - | |
| October 34 | - | 34 | 1 | - | **32** |
| .../... | | | | | |
| June 35 | - | 34 | 1 | - | **31** |
| .../... | | | | | |
| April 37 | - | 34 | 1 | - | **30** |
| .../... | | | | | |
| June 37 | - | 34 | 2 | - | **28** |
| .../... | | | | | |
| September 37 | - | 34 | 1 | - | **27** |
| .../... | | | | | |
| November 38 | - | 34 | 1 | - | **26** |
| .../... | | | | | |
| August 39 | - | 34 | 1 | - | **25** |
| .../... | | | | | |
| November 39 | - | 34 | 1 | - | **24** |
| .../... | | | | | |
| April 40 | - | 34 | - | 1 | **23** |
| May 40 | - | 34 | - | 2 | **21** |
| .../... | | | | | |
| October 40 | - | 34 | 1 | 1 | **19** |
| .../... | | | | | |
| January 41 | - | 34 | - | 1 | **18** |
| February 41 | - | 34 | - | 1 | **17** |
| .../... | | | | | |
| April 41 | - | 34 | 1 | - | **16** |
| May 41 | - | 34 | - | 1 | **15** |
| June 41 | - | 34 | - | 1 | **14** |
| .../... | | | | | |
| September 41 | - | 34 | - | 2 | **12** |
| .../... | | | | | |
| December 41 | - | 34 | - | 1 | **11** |
| January 42 | - | 34 | - | 3 | **8** |
| February 42 | - | 34 | - | 3 | **5** |
| March 42 | - | 34 | 1 | - | **4** |
| April 42 | - | 34 | - | 1 | **3** |
| May 42 | - | 34 | - | 1 | **2** |
| .../... | | | | | |
| November 42 | - | 34 | - | 1 | **1** |
| .../... | | | | | |
| June 43 | - | 34 | - | 1 | **-** |

Three quarter view of the XSF-1. The forward-firing gun installed in the upper wing can be clearly seen. (*National Archives*)

Photo showing the underwing rack installation with two 100-lb bombs. With time, the class 'S' would be altered to become 'SB' for scout-bomber when aircraft improved and were able to carry more and more ordnance. The class officially disappeared in 1946, but only one more type in the class was produced after the SF, the Curtiss SC. (*National Archives*)

## TECHNICAL DATA
### SF-1

**Manufacturer and production:**
33 by grumman Aircraft Enginneering Corporation
(Bethpage, NY)

**Type:**
Carrier-based scout aircraft

**Accomodation:**
Pilot and Observer/rear gunner.

**Power plant:**
One Wright R-1820-78 nine-cylinder radial air-cooled rated
700 hp

**Fuel & Oil**
*Fuel (US Gal):*
165 [624 l]

*Oil (US Gal):*
Standard: 8.5 [32 l]

**Dimensions:**
*Span:* 34 ft 6-in [10,52 m]
*Length:* 24 ft 0-in [7,47 m]
*Height:* 11 ft 1-in [3,38 m]
*Wing area:* 310 Sq ft [28,80 m²]

**Weights:**
*Empty:* 3,259 lb [1 478 kg]
*Gross:* 5,072 lb [2 301 kg]

**Performance:**
*Max speed:*
206 mph at 4,000 ft
[331 km/h à 700 m]

*Service ceiling:* 22,500 ft [6 850 m]

*Normal range:* 800 miles [1 285 km]

**Armament:**
1 x  fixed forward-firing 0.30-in [7.62 mm] with 500 rpg
1 x rear gun 0.30-in with 600 rounds

*provision for:*
4 x 100 lb [45 kg] bombs

Side views of the XSF-1 at Anacostia taken during autumn 1932. Except for the inscriptions written on the tail, it is difficult to identify a SF-1 from an FF at first sight especially when the left side only is displayed. (*National Archives*)

Nine SF-1s of VS-3B flying in formation. Only Red section which is leading is complete as only two aircraft each of Blue, White and Yellow sections can be seen in this photograph. (*National Archives*)

# THE UNITS

VS-3B flying in tight formation during an exercise. VS-3B was the only front-line unit to have operated the Grumman SF-1 over an 18 months period. Its withdrawal was mainly due to the lack of interest of the 'S' class after 1934. (*SDAM*)

## VS-3B

code: 3-S

*June 1934 - December 1935*

## Second line units

When the USN placed an order for 34 SF-1s, the idea was as usual to re-equip one embarked squadron. The selected unit was VS-3B aboard the USS *Lexington* and the SF-1s replaced the ageing SUs. It must be recalled that the FF-1s of VF-5B were also embarked on the same aircraft-carrier with the aim of facilitating the management of spare parts on board. By July 1934, VS-3B had received its full complement of 18 aircraft (Bu.No.9464-9482). The career of the SF-1 as an embarked aircraft was short. By December 1935, VS-3B had switched to the Vought SBU of the new class of scout-bomber created in 1934, which was corresponding to the new USN policy. The short career of the SF-1 did not however prevent accidents. The first occurred on 13 August 1934 when Bu.No.9468 was lost during a carrier deck qualification when, during the approach, the aircraft stalled at 300 feet, hit the water and sank immediately. The pilot, Enseign Kelsey, who was flying alone for this flight, was killed. Less than two months later, VS-3B had its second and last accident while flying the SF-1, killing the crew as well, Lt (jg) R.M. Patten - pilot - and RM2c J.E. Witzman - observer . This time, the squadron was in the air for tactical exercises. During the flight, Bu.No.9477 flying as 3-S-14 collided with another SF-1 (Bu.No.9471/3-S-12) causing 9477 to go into a slow nose spin, the pilot was unable to recover, crashing into the water while the other SF was able to return to the USS *Lexington*. The following month, VS-3B began to relinqush its SF-1s making a sad end of the SF-1 in an operational unit.

From the beginning, the USN was thinking to use the SF-1 in another task. Indeed, at that time, the USN needed 27 aircraft to equip an embarked squadron, 18 for the regular complement, 9 more as reserve. But the USN had placed an order for 34 SF-1s (soon reduced to 33 to convert the last one to the XSF-2) meaning the USN had about 6 SF-1s for another purpose. In conducting the various tests on the FF and SF, the USN found out the Grumman models were suit to be used as liaison aircraft for operational units. If the FF could do this ungrateful duty, the SF-1 was selected to fullfil this role because of its longer range.

Once the various tests completed, the XSF-1 served as liaison aircraft at Anacostia and was eventually re-engined with the standard dash 84 engine before to be stricken from Navy list in 1938. (*SDAM*)

As with the Grumman FF, the Grumman SF spent most of its career flying with second lines units, the reserve squadrons of the USN and USMC and this well after 1941. Here the SFs allocated to the NRAB of Oakland, California lined-up on the parking ramp.

Consequently six more SF-1s were ordered and they were actually the first to be allocated to various operational units, like VB-2B (Bu.No.9460), VF-2B (Bu.No.9461), VF-5B (Bu.No.9462), VF-6B (Bu.No.9463), while VB-5B received its SF-1 (Bu.No.9483) in June and VF3-B received its SF only in July 1934 (Bu.No.9490). While used by those units, they were also in charge of carrying out navigation and communications during squadron movements. Even in this role, the career of the SF-1 was no longer than the SF with VS-3B. Starting at the end of 1935, these liaison aircraft were withdrawn from their respective units when it was decided to use the SF-1 as main flying equipment for the reserve USN/USMC units spread out over the country. The SF-1s were soon joined by the FF-2s (see Allied Wings No.6) to reinforce the SF-1 fleet in their new role, maintenance being easy as the two aircraft were very similar.

Thus, without any kind of conversion unlike the FF-1 which were converted to FF-2s, the SF-1s were distributed amongst the various Naval Reserve Aviation Bases (NRAB), across the country. In many cases the aircraft were pooled when a USN Reserve unit and USMC reserve unit were located at the same base, flying the aircraft on alternating weekends. All SF-1s were overhauled (which included the deletion of the guns and arrester hook) and repainted. The SF-1s were assigned to various NRABs and in all they used at various moments:

Brooklyn (New York) - 5, Anacostia (DC) - 9 plus the XSF-1, Long Beach (California) - 5, Oakland (California) - 7, Seatlle (Washington) - 9, Squantum (Massachussetts) - 5, Floyd Bennett Field (New York) - 5, Opa Locka (Miami, Florida) - 3, Glenview (Chicago, Illinois) - 3, Grosse Isle (Michigan) - 1, Robertson (Missouri) - 1, Philadelphia (Pennsylvania) - 2, Minneapolis (Minessota) - 1. The aircraft were used to give refresher courses to reserve pilots or pilots temporarily posted to non-flying duties. One more (Bu.No. 9469) was also assigned to the Naval Attaché in Rio de Janeiro, Brazil between 1935 and 1938.

During the course of its career in these units, the SF-1 like the FF-2 suffered many accidents. No less than eight were recorded

between 1936 and 1940, half occurring in 1937 alone. The worst occurred on 15 June 1937, when during a ferry flight from Medford, Oregon to Pearson Flield, Washington, the plane (Bu.No.9460) crashed in fog. The pilot, Lieutenant Commander Ives, tried to find a way in a small gap but decided just after that to climb out to fly over the fog but failed. The mechanic who was seated behind was able to evacuate by parachute safely just prior the crash.

By 1941, the number of SF-1s in service had decreased steadily, only 11 were still in charge on 7 December but no more with NRABs, these SF-1s being used as liaison aircraft at various Naval Air Stations or personal aircraft of Inspectors of Naval Aviation. With the war, the surviving SF-1s were progressively withdrawn from use and the last (Bu.No.9466) was stricken from the Navy list on 15 June 1943 after a pretty discreet career with the USN.

A flight of three SF-1s assigned to NRAB Anacostia in echelon formation. Regarding markings, the reserve units applied the same rules as for the front-line units. (*National Archives*)

*Thirty-four production aircraft SF-1 ordered in November 1933 by contract 34773 (Bu.Nos 9460-9493).*

### 9460

*(c/n 154)*. **Del Anacostia 15.02.34**; Norfolk 09.03.34; Anacostia 14.03.34; San Diego Battle Force 30.03.34; VB-2B 30.04.34; San Diego Battle Force 05.04.35 for OH - completed 12.07.35; NRAB Seattle 14.08.35; NRAB Squantum 01.10.35; NRAB Seattle 15.06.37:

The pilot departed from Medford, Oregon on 15.06.37 at 1820 to deliver the aircraft to NRAB Seattle and crash occurred at 19.05 on a heavily hill, about seven miles east of Yoncella, Oregon, while the plane was enroute from Medford, Oregon to Pearson Field, Vancouver, Washington. The crash occurred while the pilot was attempting to climb back up through the fog after having made an attempt to get underneath through a small hole at the head of a small valley which was fog bound. The mechanic baled out immediately prior to the crash and just after the plane was seen be a Mr. H.R. Parks, a local farmer, to disappear into the fog in a steep climbing attitude. From an examination of the wreckage, marks on trees through which the plane passed, and evidence of eye witnesses, it is the opinion of the board that the plane stalled immediately after the mechanic jumped out and while the pilot was climbing on instruments, and that the plane crashed in the dive incident to the recovery from the stall. The plane dove through the trees at an angle of more than forty-five degrees with the horizon and came to rest within 200 yards of the point at which the mechanic landed and within three fourths of a mile from where it was seen to disappear into the fog by Mr. Parks. The wheels were retracted, the gasoline valve on upper main tank, switch on, and, from all appearance, throttle close.
The pilot was Lt.Cdr Paul F. Ives and was killed in the crash, while his passenger, AM3c Chas E. Brostrom survived. **Str-31.07.37** (536.1 TT).

### 9461

*(c/n 155)*. **Del Anacostia 19.03.34**; San Diego Battle Force 30.03.34; VF-2B the same day; San Diego Battle Force 14.01.36 for OH - completed 10.04.36; NRAB Oakland 16.04.36; NRAB Brooklyn 15.08.39:
The aircraft was damaged due to making landing with wheels in the retracted position.
The accident occurred on 13.11.39 at 10.17 on NRAB Floyd Bennett Field (NY). Note that 9461 is reported to be attached NRAB Floyd Bennett Field in the accident report, but not on movement card, but that can be explained by the fact that it was probably the turn of the Marines to fly the aircraft. The pilot was indeed a Marine, Capt. Robert W. Callaway (USMCR) and had a very few experience on the type about 10 hours only over a total flying experience exceeding 350 hours. Neither him or his passenger Pvt Frederick M. Ranichenbach (USMCR) were injured. The aircraft was not so badly damaged but it is believed that it was not economical to undertake repairs due to the high airframe hours. **Str-30.11.39.** (1,340.9 TT).

### 9462

*(c/n 156)*. **Del Anacostia 19.03.34**; San Diego Battle Force 30.03.34; VF-5B the same day; NAF 06.06.34 for OH  - completed 04.09.34; VS-3B USS *Lexington* 07.09.34; San Diego Battle Force 04.12.35 for OH - completed 05.04.36; NRAB Oakland 15.05.36; Norfolk for repairs (minor accident 20.10.36 and OH) - completed 31.12.37; NRAB Seattle 18.01.38; NAS San Diego 20.11.40; INA Consolidated date unrecorded; NAS San Diego 20.01.41 for OH - completed 31.03.41; INA Consolidated 16.04.41; NAS San  Diego 31.03.42:
Pilot was unable to raise wheels so landing was made slightly tail first. After a short run, the plane commenced turning to right. Left rudder and brake were applied to no effect and plane ground-looped. No reason could be determined for landing gear failing to raise. Brakes had just been replaced and landing gear checked on chain falls and no discrepancies observed. It is believed the pilot applied brakes too late in the turn to take effect.
The accident occurred on 28 November 1942, S-E corner of North Field (San Diego) at 11.05 during a routine check flight. The pilot, AP1c Hugh F. Graff escaped injuries. **Str-31.12.42**.

### 9463

*(c/n 157)*. **Del Anacostia 19.03.34**; San Diego Battle Force 30.03.34; VF-6B the same day; San Diego Battle Force for OH 24.12.35 - completed 18.03.36; NRAB Long Beach 19.03.36:
The plane was taking off as No.2 of a section on North-South runway at Municipal Airport, Long Beach (CA), taking off in a southerly direction. Plane swerved to left and collided with a Government owned station wagon parked at edge of field approximately 140 feet from east edge of runway and 1,000 feet from start of take-off. Engine broke loose on impact. Fire broke out immediately and progressed rapidly but without explosion, resulting in destruction of the aircraft. Personnel had sufficient time to get clear ahead of advance of fire. Other two planes completed take-off successfully.
The crash took place at 13.37 on 08.08.39 and the aircraft was totally destroyed by fire. The pilot, Lt (jg) W.S Carroll (USNR) was

After having served as utility aircraft for VB-2B in 1934-1935, Bu.No.9460 was allocated to various Reserve squadrons. The aircraft was overhauled at San Diego when it received new markings which include the Navy/Marines reserve insignia on the fuselage and the Reserve squadron bands on the rudder. Note the inverted chevron on the upper wings, however its colour cannot be identified with certainty. It is believed that this photo was taken on completion of the overhaul in July 1935 before being allocated to any NRAB as no individual number is visible nor colours on the cowling.

Bu.No.9461 was assigned to VF-2B as utility aircraft in March 1934 and became 2-F-19 (i.e. the 19th aircraft of the squadron). It not clear when this photo was taken, and there is no obvious reason why the Bu.No. has been deleted. Note that this aircraft has no squadron insignia painted on, another oddity but had on the other hand the gunnery trophy pennant painted under the cockpit! The tail colour of VF-2B was Lemon yellow.

As for Bu.No.9461, Bu.No.9463 began its career with the USN in serving as utility aircraft with VF-6B until December 1935. Here, the aircraft has received the full squadron markings, like the Pat Sullivan's 'Felix the Cat' and the white tail and horizontal tail. VF-6B was embarked on the USS Saratoga at that time. An inscription is written under the pilot's cockpit but is totally illegible. It was probably the rank and name of the pilot.

Bu.No.9464 was the fifth production SF-1 but was the first to be allocated to VS-3B on the USS *Lexington*. This photo seems to have been retouched and surprisingly the tail has its regular colour for the squadron - Yellow - not painted on. However, as being the Red section's leader, it wore the right markings with the red fuselage band and red cowling.

Bu.No.9466 had a long career with the USN. First with VS-3B then with NRAB Long Beach in California and then as utility aircraft at various Naval Air Bases. It was offcially stricken from the Navy list in June 1943 even if its current status in 1943 remains uncertain. 9466 is seen early in its career with NRAB Long Beach with the reserve stripes painted on the rudder. It received also the individual number '4' painted on a white fuselage band and the cowling has been painted in white as well. Logically, 9466 should have also a white reverted chevron painted on the upper wings with a black number.

Bu.No.9467 seen while serving with VS-3B in 1934-1935. 9467 was the second aircraft of the Blue Section, and the tail is painted yellow. Contrary to some most USN aircraft types at that time, the SF-1s were not assigned sequentially. It was later assigned to NRAB Oakland and Brooklyn before ending its days as instructional airframe at Chicago. Note the meritorious pennant painted forward the cockpit.

slightly injured and the passenger Sea2C T.B. Burnham (USNR) escaped injuries. The pilto was an experienced pilot with over 2,500 hours logged but onlt 13 on type. **Str-31.08.39**. (1,004.8 TT)

## 9464

*(c/n 158)*. **Del Anacostia 12.04.34**; Norfolk Battle Force 01.06.34; VS-3B 29.06.34; San Diego Battle Force 02.04.35 for OH - completed 12.07.35; NRAB Seattle 14.08.35; San Diego for modifications 25.10.35; NRAB Floyd Bennett Field 06.11.35; NAF 15.07.37 for OH - completed 07.12.37; NRAB Long Beach 28.12.37; NRAB Opa Locka 26.08.39. **Str-31.08.40**. (897.4 TT).

## 9465

*(c/n 159)*. **Del Anacostia 21.04.34** for Norfolk Battle Force; VS-3B USS *Lexington* 02.07.34; San Diego Battle Force 16.11.34 for OH - completed 25.01.35; VS3-B USS *Lexington* 19.02.35; San Diego Battle Force 20.11.35 for OH - completed 25.01.36; NRAB Seatlle 08.02.36; NAS San Diego 03.05.38 for OH - completed 28.11.38; NRAB Seattle; NRAB Opa Locka 17.08.39; NRAB Anacostia 14.07.40. **Str-31.10.40**.

## 9466

*(c/n 160)*. **Del Anacostia 21.04.34** for Norfolk Battle Force; VS-3B 29.06.34; San Diego 21.01.36 for OH - completed 27.07.36; NRAB Long Beach 31.07.36; Norfolk 10.08.36 for OH (minor accident) - completed 04.12.36; NRAB Long Beach 09.12.36; NAS San Diego 19.12.40 for OH - completed 06.06.41; San Diego (Operational) 16.06.41; NAS Alameda 02.05.42. **Str-15.06.43**.

## 9467

*(c/n 161)*. **Del Anacostia 21.04.34** for Norfolk Battle Force; VS-3B 29.06.34; San Diego Battle Force 17.12.35 for OH - completed 02.05.36; NRAB Oakland 29.05.36; NRAB Brooklyn 22.10.39; NAF for Project 'F' 20.03.41. **Str-30.05.42**. Became instructional or display airframe at NRAB Chicago.

## 9468

*(c/n 162)*. **Del Anacostia 10.05.34** for Norfolk Battle Force; VS3-B 02.07.34:

During carrier deck qualification, the pilot attempted to short a turn, preparatory to entering landing groove at about stalling speed. The aircraft went into a left and tail spin from an altitude of about 300 feet. The pilot made a partial recovery, the airplane striking the water head on at an angle of about 60 degrees. It sank immediately, within an estimated time of between thirty seconds and one minute. The pilot was either stunned by the impact or killed outright, as no movement was detected inside the plane either before or after sinking. There was no evidence to indicate that the flotation gear of the plane has been operated.

The accident tool place on 13.08.34 at 12.58 at sea. The pilot, Ensign J.H. Kelsey (USN) was killed. He had flown only 49 hours on SF-1s. **Str-29.09.34** (49.6 TT).

## 9469

*(c/n 163)*. **Del Anacostia 10.05.34** for Norfolk Battle Force; VS3-B 02.07.34; San Diego Battle Force 12.06.35 for OH - completed 10.10.35; Naval Attaché Rio de Janeiro (Brasil) 15.10.35; NAS Norfolk for OH 22.09.38 - completed 05.05.39; NRAB Squantum 14.05.39; INA Vought-Sikorsky 19.10.40; NAS Jacksonville 05.01.42. **Str-06.01.42.** (761.3 TT).

## 9470

*(c/n 164)*. **Del Anacostia 10.05.34** for Norfolk Battle Force; VS-3B 29.06.34; San Diego Battle Force 21.11.34 for OH (minor accident) - completed 19.04.35; VS-3B USS *Lexington* 16.04.35; San Diego Battle Force 11.12.35 for OH - completed 23.02.36; NRAB Anacostia (VN-6R) 06.03.36; NAF for OH 25.05.37 - completed 29.01.38; NRAB Anacostia 01.02.38. **Str-31.05.40** (1,691.7 TT). NYA Columbus (SC) for display or instructional airframe 30.06.40.

## 9471

*(c/n 165)*. **Del Anacostia 10.05.34** for Norfolk Battle Force; Norfolk Battle Force 14.06.34; VS-3B 02.07.34; NAF 16.07.34; VS-3B USS *Lexington* 01.09.34; San Diego Battle Force for OH 01.10.35 - completed 20.12.35; NRAB Seattle 23.12.35; San Diego for repairs 09.01.36 - completed 18.03.36; NRAB Seattle 21.03.36:

About forty minutes after take-off, the pilot noticed flames breaking forth from the engine section, sweeping back outside of fuselage to the vicinity of the after cockpit. He immediately instructed the mechanic in the rear cockpit to jump. He then felt a jar on the plane, looked back and observed that the mechanic was out and the parachute opened. The fire subsided, evidently due to the action of the fire extinguisher. The pilot started a spiral with the reported intention of landing alongside of the mechanic. At an altitude of about 1,000 feet, fire again broke out and the pilot jumped. His parachute opened and about twenty minutes later he was rescued from the water by a civilian tug summoned to the spot by accompanying aircraft.

It is believed that the jar on the plane felt by the pilot, was undoubtedly the impact of the mechanic against the tail surfaces of the plane. This opinion is supported by the statement of the pilot of the accompanying aircraft, who observed the mechanic rise in his seat immediately after the outbreak of the fire, his parachute streaming from the cockpit and passing beneath the tail surfaces of the airplane. It is believed that the action of the parachute dragged the mechanic from the cockpit and threw him against some part of the tail surface. The plane, after having been abandoned by the pilot, dove into the water at a point about two miles from Port Townsend Light.

This accident occurred on 12.09.37 at 14.00 and was flown by Capt. Joseph P. Adams (USMCR) who survived. However, his passenger, Technical Sergeant John F. Bilsborrow (USMCR) was killed. Capt Adams was a very experienced pilot with over 1,000 hours already logged. **Str-30.10.37.** (791.9 TT).

### 9472

*(c/n 166)*. **Del Anacostia 11.05.34** for Norfolk Battle Force; VS-3B 02.07.34; NAF 21.12.35 for OH - completed 10.06.36; NRAB Squantum 16.06.36; NAF 22.12.36; NRAB Squantum 11.02.37; NRAB Anacostia 08.06.37; NRAB Squantum 09.08.39; INA Pratt & Whitney 19.10.40; NAF for disposition. **Str-30.09.41** (1,106.3 TT). Became instruciional airframe at Naval Reserve Training School 16.02.42.

### 9473

*(c/n 167)*. **Del Norfolk Battle Force 16.05.34**; VS-3B 02.07.34; San Diego for repairs date illegible; Naval Attaché, Rio (Brasil), date unrecorded. NRAB Grosse Isle 19.09.35; NRAB Anacostia (VN-6R) 06.03.36; NAF 21.05.37; NRAB Anacostia 15.06.37; NRAB Glenview 07.08.38; NRAB Anacostia 14.11.38; NRAB Brooklyn 12.08.39.

The airplane taxied nomrally, but on the take-oof the right landing gear felt as though it suddenly gave way. The right wing dropped and the airplane started to swerve to the right. Full throttle was required to straighten the plane out and stall it off. When the gear was cranked up only the left wheel came up. When the gear was cranked down the left wheel worked normally but the right wheel remained stationary. The plane landed in water alongside a motor boat.

The accident occurred on 10.10.40 at 11.00. The crew, pilot Ens. Robert A. Winston (USNR) and AMM3c Emilio J. Marrone escaped of any injuries. Because the plane laid under salt water, the aircraft was not repaired. **Str-30.04.41.** (1,271.6 TT).

### 9474

*(c/n 168)*. **Del Norfolk Battle Force 16.05.34**; VS-3B 02.07.34; San Diego Battle Force 25.11.35 for OH - completed 10.02.36; NRAB Floyd Bennett Field 22.02.36:

While on a flight from Floyd Bennett Field to NAS Norfolk, the plane began to run very low on fuel and the pilot, knowing that he could not reach Langley, looked for a field in which to land. He flew over the Rappahannrock River and finally found a field with wheet stacked in it and it samed firm and sufficiently smooth for a safe landing. After dragging the field, he landed and first checked its position with the corner, the decided to go on to either Dahlgren or to milford because the field, already softened by the rains of the previous day, would become too soft for a take-off if rain should again fall upon it. The first attempt to take off was a failure and the pilot cut the gun. He tried a second take-off. As he was about to rise, the wheels struck softer ground, yet the wheels left the ground, probably because the pilot over-controlled in trying to prevent a nove-over. There was insufficant speed, however and he cut the gun in attempt to prevent a crash into the embarkment at the end of the field. The ship landed less than 100 feet from the bank, and went right on into it, turning over on its back.

The accident occurred on 19.06.37 at 10.30, the pilot, Ens. S. deLima was sligtly injured. The aircarft was salvaged and sent to NAS Norfolk but was eventually not repaired. **Str-31.07.37** (692.3 TT).

### 9475

*(c/n 169)*. **Del Anacostia 28.05.34** for Norfolk Battle Force; VS-3B 02.07.34, Norfolk Battle Force 11.09.34 for OH - completed 07.08.35; Norfolk Reserves 29.03.35; NRAB Anacostia (VN-6R) 13.08.35; NAF 18.05.38; NRAB Anacostia 26.07.38; NRAB Roberston 17.11.38; NRAB Philadelphia 20.08.39; NRAB Anacostia 06.09.39. **Str-31.05.40**. (956.4 TT). NRAB New York for exhibition at the World Fair 30.06.40.

### 9476

*(c/n 170)*. **Del Anacostia 28.05.34** for Norfolk Battle Force; VS-3B 02.07.34; San Diego Battle Force for OH - completed 10.02.36; NRAB Oakland 13.02.36; San Diego Battle Force 21.03.41. **Str-31.01.42.** (2,133.7 TT). Went to NAS Alamelda for test ground.

### 9477

*(c/n 171)*. **Del Norfolk Battle Force 31.05.34**; VS-3B Lexington. On 30.10.34 at 08.52 the aircraft was lost in an accident at sea:
The squadron was at about 2,500 feet altitude in Division 'V-of-V's' with the Second Division about 500 feet behind and 300 feet above the First Division. The Second Division was composed of the Fourth Section, planes 10, 11, 12, the Fifth Section, planes 13 and 14, and the Sixth Section, planes 15 and 16. The Second Division Leader observed the First Division proceed into or behind a cloud bank on the starboard hand, and made a 45 to 60 degrees banked trun to the left to avoid the cloud. No.12 in the Fourth Section pulled up to permit the Fifth Section to cross over if necessary. The Fifth Section was unable to remain on the inside of the

The exact date this photo was taken is not known but probably around 1937-1938. So it is not possible to know with which unit Bu.No.9473 was serving as No.1, could be NRAB Glenview or Brooklyn. When applied the markings of the Reserve units had normally to follow the rules of the front-line units. Hence as No.1, Bu.No.9473 had a red fuselage band and cowling. The tail is believed to be painted in red.

Bu.No.9473 most of its career at NRAB Anacostia where it became No.4. As No.4, Bu.No.9473 had a white fuselage band and cowling. However, the digit '4' on the cowling was an unofficial practice used by Reserve units. The tail is believed to be painted in blue.
(*William T. Larkins*)

Bu.No.9474 belongs to the first batch assigned to VS-3B and became 3-S-11. The use of the SF-1 with VS-3B was short, but long enough to obtain the meritorious and wanted 'E' which is painted just below the cockpit with the associated pennant (orange with a circular black centre). Coded 11, this SF-1 is the No.2 of the Fourth Section and has its upper cowling painted in black.

Bu.No.9476 was assigned to VS-3B on 02.07.34 as aircraft of the leader of the Fifth Section - colour Willow Green. Note the machine-gun installed on the upper wing, meaning that the squadron was probably doing some manoeuvers when this photo was taken. Note the pennant located forward of the cockpit, probably the pennant for excellence and not the Gunnery trophy reserved for fighter units.

Something pretty rare for a USN aircraft in 1936, a lack of paint, leaving this SF-1 in Natural Metal Finish. Bu.No.9481 is seen here serving as No.2 of NRAB Long Beach (confirmed by the inscription painted on the reserve insignia). Otherwise the remaining markings follow the regulations, with the upper cowling painted in red with a thin black line, and the standard reserve stripes painted on the rudder.

Bu.No.9483 was assigned to VB-5B as utility aircraft for the squadron. As such it was allocated the number 19 reserved for this kind of task. Note the squadron insignia painted well forward on the fuselage near the engine cowling. It was a unusual location compared to the BF2C which equipped the squadron in 1934-1935 - see Allied Wings No.11.

turn and pulled across the Fourth Section. He lost the Fourth under him and did not clear them with the wing plane which collided with No.12 so that his right wing was forward of No.12's left wing which struck No.14's fuselage. The right wingtip of No.14 was knowcked off or chewed off by the propeller up to the outboard struts. No.12's left wing tip and his engine ring cowling and propeller were damaged. Both planes disengaged almost immediately. No.14 went into a slow nose down spin from which it appeared to straighten out once, but from which it did not revover and crashed in the water. No one was observed to get clear of the plane. Lt (jg) R.M. Patten, (USN), pilot and RM2c J.E. Witzman (USN), observer were both posted missing. **Str-30.11.34**.

### 9478

(c/n 172). **Del Norfolk Battle Force 31.05.34**; VS-3B 02.07.34; San Diego for OH 16.04.35 - completed 09.08.35; NRAB Seattle 14.08.35; San Diego for changes 10.10.35; NRAB Seattle 13.10.35; San Diego for minor repairs 16.07.36 - completed 18.11.36; NRAB Seattle 09.12.36; NRAB Anacostia 09.10.40; NAF (VX-3D4) 17.10.40. **St-28.02.42**.

### 9479

(c/n 173). **Del Norfolk Battle Force 08.06.34**; VS-3B 27.06.34; San Diego Battle Force for OH 01.11.35 - completed 25.01.36; NRAB Long Beach 27.01.36; NRAB Philadelphia 29.08.39; NAF (VX-3D4) 25.10.40. **St-31.12.41**. Became instructional airframe at NRAB Glenview.

### 9480

(c/n 174). **Del Norfolk Battle Force 08.06.34**; VS-3B 28.06.34; San Diego Battle Force for OH 16.08.35 - completed 10.11.35; NRAB Long Beach 13.11.35; NAS San Diego (Operational) 23.10.40; San Diego Battle Force 05.11.40 for OH - completed 15.07.41; San Diego (Operational) 05.02.42. **Str-28.02.42** (1,220.4 TT). Became instructional airframe at NAS Almenada 24.04.42.

### 9481

(c/n 175). **Del Norfolk Battle Force 08.06.34**; VS-3B 29.06.34; San Diego for OH 16.12.35 - completed 21.04.36; NRAB Long Beach 06.05.36; NRAB Minneapolis 14.03.39; NRAB Opa Locka 08.01.39; San Diego Battle Force 22.11.40; USS *Saratoga* 26.11.40; San Diego Battle Force 26.12.40. **Str-31.01.41.** (1,222.6 TT).

### 9482

(c/n 176). **Del Norfolk Battle Force 08.06.34**; VF-5B 30.06.34; San Diego Battle Force for OH 20.12.35 - completed 09.03.36; NRAB Anacostia (VN-6R) 17.03.36; NAF 10.08.36; NRAB Anacostia 24.03.37; INA Curtiss 17.10.40; Norfolk 29.01.41. **Str-30.04.42**.

### 9483

(c/n 177). **Del Anacostia 23.06.34** for Norfolk Battle Force; VB-5B 26.06.34; USS *Ranger* VB-5B 15.08.34; USS *Lexington* 08.10.34; San Diego Battle Force 21.01.36 probably for OH; NRAB Seattle 07.08.36; NAS San Diego 09.01.39 for OH - completed 17.05.39; NRAB Seattle 25.05.39; NAS Alameda 17.10.40. **Str-28.02.41** due to cost of OH. (950.7 TT).

### 9484

(c/n 178). **Del Anacostia 23.06.34** for Norfolk Battle Force; VS-3B USS Lexington 16.08.34; San Diego Battle Force for 17.12.35 - completed 08.05.36; Norfolk 24.01.36; NRAB Floyd Bennett Field 22.05.36; NRAB Seattle 24.08.37; NAS San Diego for OH 18.10.38 - completed 14.02.39; NRAB Seattle 21.02.39; NRAB Brooklyn 23.08.39; NAS Jacksonville for disposition 22.04.41. **Str-31.05.41** (1,254.1 TT).

### 9485

(c/n 179). **Del Anacostia 22.06.34** for Norfolk Battle Force; VS-3B USS *Lexington* 16.08.34; San Diego Battle Force for OH 25.11.35 - completed 10.02.36; NRAB Squantum 26.02.36; NRAB Oakland 16.06.37; San Diego Battle Force 21.03.41; NAS San Pedro 01.04.41:
On 16 April, during a familiarisation flight, the pilot, AMM1c James K. Marshall (USN) made a normal landing but he allowed the aircraft to ground loop to left. The right wheel consequently crushed. It was 10.20. The pilot and the passenger, ACMM James J; Wagner escaped any injuries.
The aircraft was sent to San Diego Battle Force 22.04.41 for inspection but was declared beyond economical repair due to its age. **Str-30.01.41.** (1504.3 TT). Became instructional airframe at NAS Jacksonville 24.06.41.

## 9486

*(c/n 180)* **Del San Diego Battle Force 16.06.34**; VS-3B 24.04.35; San Diego for OH 16.12.35 - completed 16.01.36; NRAB Squantum 25.01.36; NRAB Oakland 16.06.37; NRAB Brooklyn 17.08.39; NAS Quonset Point 17.10.40 (temporray assigment); NRAB Squantum 20.12.40; NAF 10.02.41; INA Baltimore to be stricken 23.05.41; NRAB Glenview 18.01.42. **Str-31.01.42.**

## 9487

*(c/n 181)* **Del San Diego Battle Force 05.07.34**; USS *Lexington* (VS-3B??); San Diego for OH 17.06.35 - completed 09.08.35. NRAB Oakland 14.08.35; NAS San Diego for OH 09.10.36 - completed 31.12.36; NRAB Oakland 04.01.37; NAS Alamelda 06.11.40. **Str-28.02.42.**

## 9488

*(c/n 182)* **Del San Diego Battle Force 11.07.34**; Norfolk Battle Force for VS-3B USS *Lexington* 10.09.34; San Diego Battle Force 17.12.35; Norfolk for OH 24.01.36 - completed 30.04.36; NRAB Floyd Bennett Field 08.05.36; NRAB Anacostia 03.08.37; NAF (VX4-D4) 17.10.40. Ens. J.R. Thomas was ready to go for a test flight on 25.03.42 when an accident occurred at 14.00 on Mustin Field: The pilot left the plane without chocks but with engine running. Parking brakes were not installed on this type plane. The brakes on the airplane could not be operated from rear cockpit. Engine speed revolutions at idle speed were sufficient to start plane moving, with result the plane ran free and crashed into portable equipment in the immediate vicinity.
Due to the age of the aircraft no repairs were undertook. **Str-30.04.42.**

## 9489

*(c/n 183)* **Del 06.07.34**; San Diego Battle Force 16.07.34; VB-2B USS *Saratoga*; San Diego Battle Force for OH - completed 10.01.36; NRAB Floyd Bennett Field 28.01.36:
The pilot landed successfully in a small emergency field due to improper operation of the fuel supply system. This was the basic cause of the ensuing accident. After refueling, the plane on taking off hit a small tree causing it to crash. On the take-off, after being in the air a few feet, the plane settled back on for no definitely assignable reason, which prolonged the take-off and caused the failure to clear the tree.
The accident occurred on 23.04.37 at 16.10 near Oneca (CN), and the pilot, Lt (jg) Roy H. Callahan - USNR - was not injured. **Str-29.05.37.** (391.7 TT).

## 9490

*(c/n 184)* **Del 06.07.37**; Norfolk Battle Force for VF-3B 10.07.34; VF-2B 11.09.34; San Diego Battle Force VF-3B 20.11.34; San Diego Battle for OH 10.01.36 - completed 08.05.36; Norfolk 21.01.36; NRAB Squantum 19.05.36; NRAB Long Beach 22.06.37; NAS San Diego (Operational) 23.10.40. **Str-20.09.41.**

## 9491

*(c/n 185)* **Del 12.07.34**; San Diego Battle Force 19.07.34; Norfolk Battle Force for VS-3B 10.09.34; San Diego Battle 17.12.35; Norfolk for OH 24.01.36 - completed 03.06.36; NRAB Floyd Bennett Field 16.06.36; NRAB Long Beach 20.08.37; NRAB Glenview for major OH 06.03.39; NRAB Minneapolis 11.05.39; NRAB Squantum 08.08.39; NAS Jacksonville 26.05.41. **Str-30.06.41.** (1,048.5 TT).

## 9492

*(c/n 186)* **Del 12.07.34**; San Diego Battle Force 19.07.34; VS-3B USS *Lexington* 22.03.35; San Diego Battle Force for OH 17.12.35 - completed 25.12.35; NRAB Oakland 29.01.36; San Diego for OH 24.11.36 - completed 18.02.37; NRAB Oakland 26.02.37.
The airplane crashed into San Fransisco Bay one mile south east of San Mateo Bridge, resulting in instantaneaous death to the pilot and severe injuries to the passenger. The plane was found floating with both flotation bags inflated. Subsequent examiniation of the wreckage disclosed that the flotation bottle had shifted forward in its compartment, actuating the cutter valve.
The accident occured on 19.06.35 at 11.46, the pilot, Lt William M. Holsenbeck (USNR) was killed while the passenger Robert A. May survived. **Str-15.02.39.** (791.2 TT).

## 9493

*(c/n 187)* **Del as XSF-2 Anacostia 03.12.34** (but officially accepted by the Navy on 05.11.35); Norfolk 04.03.35; Anacostia 15.03.35; Grumman Corp. 27.05.35; Anacostia 22.06.35; Langley Field 02.12.35; Anacostia 10.01.36; Norfolk for OH 17.08.36 - completed 04.02.37; Anacostia 09.02.37; NAF for OH 17.05.39 - completed 19.01.40; Anacostia 22.01.40; NAS Norfolk for Mechanic school 18.03.41. **Str-31.03.41.** (1,866.2 TT).

Bu.No.9485 on finals with gear down about to land. This SF-1 was assigned first to NRAB Squantum after its service with VS-3B then to NRAB Oakland. The NRAB Oakland insignia is clearly visible and 9485 became number 10 with the associated markings - black fuselage band (white thin band outlined) and the cowling painted in black.
(*William T. Larkins*)

Bu.No.9486 was first stored at San Diego for almost one year and was assigned to VS-3B in April 1935 only. Here it became the aircraft of the leader of the Fourth Section with its black markings. Later it was overhauled to serve with the Reserve squadrons and was finally stricken from the Navy list in January 1942.

Bu.No.9487 was first stored after acceptance by the Navy and then served briefly with VS-3B in 1935 to make up attrition. It was overhauled and then assigned to NRAB Oakland where this photo was taken. The markings are conventional with the Navy/USMC reserve insignia painted on the fuselage, the individual number painted in the middle of the fuselage and the corresponding cowling markings (upper part painted in white) and the rudder painted with the Reserve colours. The wheels are also painted in white, a common practice in Reserve units.
By the and of its career it served as #2 at NAS Alameda with very simple markings and on Natural Metal Finish.
(*William T. Larkins*)

Bu.No.9490 never served with the VS-3B but as utility aircraft (left with the VF-3B on USS *Ranger* with a green tail) or with reserve units during all its career see below.

Bu.No.9490 seen from two different angles while serving at NRAB Long Beach at the end of the thirties. Note the NRAB Long Beach insignia and the rudder painted with the reserve units colours and the white cowling.

Above, the XSF-2 while conducting a flight test during winter 1934-1935 and below a three-quarter view of the same aircraft taken at Anacostia. Even if the tests were satisfactory, no production was ordered afterwards and Bu.No.9493 remained the only one of its kind. (*National Archives*)

Right the two sides of the XSF-2 at the end of its career at Anacostia, painted in light grey.

Above the XSF-1 taken more or less at the same time and same place left in Natural Metal Finish. Differences between the two prototypes can be easily noticed.
(*William T. Larkins*)

Another view of SFs allocated to the NRAB of Oakland, California lined-up on the parking ramp - see page 8. Only a simple fence was considered as enough as to prevent intrusion!

†

ROLL OF HONOUR

*SF-1*

| Name | Rank | Origin | Date | BuNo |
|------|------|--------|------|------|
| **BILSBORROW**, J.F. | T/Sgt | USMCR | 12.09.37 | 9471 |
| **HOLSENBECK**, W.M. | Lt | USNR | 19.06.35 | 9492 |
| **IVES**, P.F. | Lt.Cdmr | USN | 15.06.37 | 9460 |
| **KELSEY**, J.H. | Ens. | USN | 13.08.34 | 9468 |
| **PATTEN**, R.M. | Lt (jg) | USN | 30.10.34 | 9477 |
| **WITZMAN**, J.E. | RM2c | USNR | 30.10.34 | 9477 |

*Total: 6*

Two Grumman SF-1s, Bu.9474 and Bu.9476 in 1935 while serving with VS-3B on USS *Lexington*. See p14 and p15 respectively for details. Contrary to some most USN aircraft types at that time, the SF-1s were not assigned sequentially.

## Squadron Section Colours

**First**
*(Insignia Red)*

Aircraft #1

Aircraft #2

Aircraft #3

**Third**
*(True Blue)*

Aircraft #7

Aircraft #8

Aircraft #9

**Fifth**
*(Willow Green)*

Aircraft #13

Aircraft #14

Aircraft #15

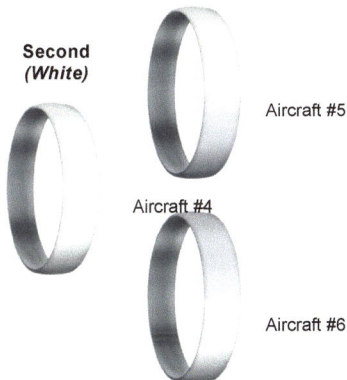

**Second**
*(White)*

Aircraft #4

Aircraft #5

Aircraft #6

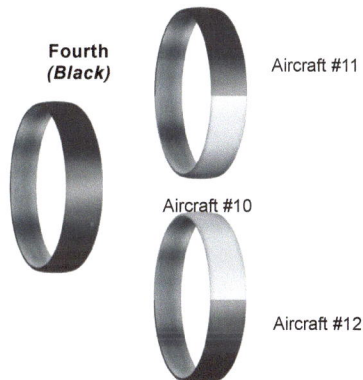

**Fourth**
*(Black)*

Aircraft #10

Aircraft #11

Aircraft #12

**Sixth**
*(Lemon Yellow)*

Aircraft #16

Aircraft #17

Aircraft #18

**(Aircraft of the leaders (#1, 4, 7, 10, 13, 16) were also identified with a fuselage band painted at the colour of the Section**

Above, Bu.No.9460, the first production SF-1 was the utility aircraft of VB-2B in 1934 which was assigned to the USS *Saratoga*.
Left, same allocation for Bu.No.9463 - see p.10 - allocated to the VF-6B on the USS *Saratoga*, and below Bu.No.9483 on USS *Ranger* (VB-5B) - see p.15.
Note the lack of cowling paint, a regular practice for all utility aircraft, here coded '19'.

Above, Bu.No.9490 of the VF-3B on USS *Ranger* in 1934 - see p.19.
After one year of operational service, the surviving SF-1s were issued to various Reserve units after overhaul. From that time, the arrester hook became useless and was deleted. Left Bu.No.9466 assigned to NRAB Long Beach and below also issued to NRAB Long Beach Bu.No.9481, but left in Natural Metal Finish, an unusual practice in the late thirties - see p.15. At Long Beach, the SF-1s were normally assigned to the VN-13RD11, which was one of the three USN and USMC units based there.

Above, another SF-1 of NRAB Long Beach. The Reserve insignia was replaced by a unit insignia - see p.19. The Reserve units painted their aircraft with various markings like Bu.9487 of NRAB Oakland which had its wheels painted in red matching with the colour of the Section (below), while Bu.No.9485 (left), is closer of the USN front line units regulations even if both served in the same reserve unit, the VN-14RD12 - see p.18. The other reserve unit of NRAB Oakland was the VO-8MR of the USMC.

The Reverve rudder stripes were progressively replaced by various tail colours which seems to have evoluated during the years. Above Bu.No.9473 with a red tail and believed to be the first makings painted on this SF-1 when issued to NRAB Anacostia (VN-6R) - p.14. After overhaul, it was re-issued to NRAB Anacostia with a blue tail and the Reserve insignia painted in the forward part of the fuselage (below - p.8) later replaced with a unit insignia (right - p.14). Whether or not these reserve unit insignias were official is not known.

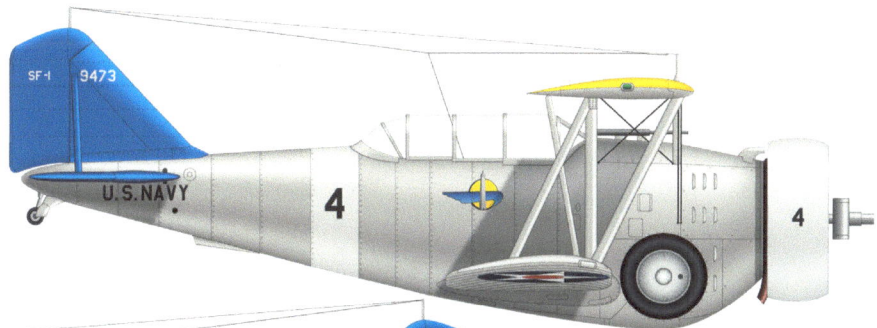

# SQUADRONS!

**No.3**

The Supermarine
**SPITFIRE Mk. V**
in the Far East

**SQUADRONS!**

**No.7**

The Supermarine
**SPITFIRE F.21**

Phil H. LISTEMANN

Vol. 2:
Type Designation
'A'
(Pt-2)

**USN 192...**

RAF, Dominion & Allied Squadrons
at War:
Study, History and Statistics

No.309 (Polish) Squadron
1940 - 1947

**SQUADRONS!**

**No.2**

Republic
Thunderbolt Mk.I

# www.RAF-IN-COMBAT.com

- USN Aircraft 1922-1962 -
- Squadrons! -
- RAF, Dominion and Allied squadrons at War -
- Allied Wings -
- Famous squadrons of WW2 -

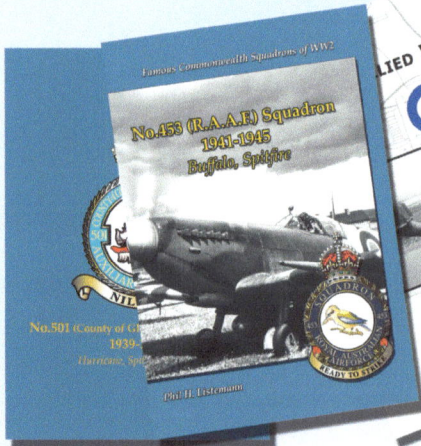

Famous Commonwealth Squadrons of WW2

No.453 (R.A.A.F) Squadron
1941-1945
Buffalo, Spitfire

No.501 (County of G...)
1939...
Harricane, Sp...

Phil H. Listemann

RAF, Dominion & Allied Squa...
at War:
Study, History and Stati...

No.131 (County of Kent) S...
1941 - 1945

**ALLIED WINGS**

**ALLIED WINGS**

**ALLIED WINGS**

Short SINGAPORE III

The Supermarine SPITFIRE
F.24

The Curtiss SB2C In
French service...

www.ingramcontent.com/pod-product-compliance
Lightning Source LLC
LaVergne TN
LVHW072123070426

835511LV00002B/75